MW00945479

OUTSMART

THE

UNEXPECTED

OUTSMART

THE

UNEXPECTED:

Grow Your Creativity the Edge-of-your-seat Way

Regina Pacelli

ISBN 1440477914

EAN-13 9781440477911

TABLE OF CONTENTS

"Never tell me the odds!"
- Han Solo, 'Star Wars: Episode V
The Empire Strikes Back', 1980

*"We dance around in a ring and suppose.
The secret sits in the middle and knows."*
- Robert Frost, The Secret Sits from
'A Witness Tree', 1942

*"No more talking. No more guessing. Don't even
think about nothing that's not right in front of
you. That's the real challenge. You've gotta save
yourselves from yourselves."*
- Rennes, 'Cube', 1997

WELCOME

Stuff happens. It's one of the immutable laws of life. So, the better prepared you are to deal with the unexpected, potentially life altering events that will inevitably come your way, the better off you'll be. The more 'shock proof' and nimble-minded you become, the more you will be able to achieve a successful outcome and to do it with the least amount of stress and negative impact on your well-being.

Shocks and unexpected events, happy and horrible, minor and extreme, happen to someone, somewhere every day. The sinking of the titanic, for instance, is an extreme example. The passengers on the titanic were from all walks of life. They were wealthy families relaxing and enjoying an ocean voyage. They were immigrants focused on the new life their destination promised. They were all preoccupied in one way or another. That their lives would soon be in peril was the furthest thing from their mind.

Likewise, the employees, all from a diverse spectrum of trades and professions, skills and knowledge, arriving at the World Trade Center the day of the 9/11 attack, did not expect that their lives would be in jeopardy a short while later.

Of course, all unexpected events are not of the extreme, life-threatening variety just described above, but how you react to the unforeseen, life-changing events or lesser predicaments that you can suddenly come face to face with, the choices that you make, your ability to think on your feet and come up with ideas and think things through, can have a very real impact on your future.

Even unexpected events of a less extreme variety, such as noticing a suspicious stranger following you, being offered a job you didn't apply for, getting falsely accused of something, or just being visited by someone important to your future at a very inopportune time can have very different outcomes depending on how you handle those events. You don't always have the luxury of time to figure out what to do. You don't always have much information either. Helping the characters in each of the cliffhangers in *Outsmart the Unexpected* to resolve the situations they find themselves in will in turn help you to become an even more creative, quick thinking problem solver.

There are no absolute rules of the road or guidelines here, but I can offer some suggestions. Each of the stories gives clues about the characters' abilities, personality, and/or life situation. Sometimes those clues are sparse, irrelevant, or misleading. In coming up with a solution to their predicament, think - what would/could 'they' do based on what you know about them? What would you do - the same thing or something different?

How many solutions can you come up with that will likely achieve a successful outcome and a happy ending for the character(s)? What solutions or courses of action would make a bad situation worse? Also, see Appendix A - Ideas for taking *Outsmart the Unexpected* beyond the borders of the book.

Some of the stories are pretty far out there (my penchant for tales with a twist I guess). I hope you have as much enjoyment reading and solving them as I had writing them.

Wishing you warm, breezy days, and successful outcomes,

Regina Pacelli

THE CLIFFHANGERS

Bigger than a Bread Box

It was with eager anticipation that Maxwell opened the large box that was on the table before him. He was so excited to get at what lay inside that he didn't even think to use a knife or scissors to assist him in opening the box, but rather, just clawed at the wrapping until the contents were revealed. Within the box was a collection of a dozen or so obscure books that Maxwell had managed to discover in his research on the Internet. One of them surely had to contain the answer he was desperately searching for.

He could find no information on the Internet or any of the other possible information sources he could think of such as the local universities, public libraries, or bookstores. What was worse, due to the nature of the problem, he didn't feel he could let anyone know, which closed off that avenue of assistance to him. He especially did not want his wife or two young sons to know what had happened and took great pains to prevent them from finding out. His wife had told him many times about her fears concerning his experiments, one time becoming quite agitated when he felt it a necessary precaution to build a specially designed sub-basement in their house to conduct them in. Now, after his wife's fearful fantasies had materialized into an alarming and terrible reality, he did not want to appear foolish to her, the neighbors, his colleagues at the university, or to anyone else for that matter.

So, Maxwell forged ahead, trying to find a solution. He was bright. If there was a solution, and for everyone's sake, he knew there better be one, he'd figure one out. He'd figure out a way to contain it before it got completely out of control. Besides, if his superiors at the university ever found out, he suspected that he'd probably lose his position and not be able to work elsewhere as a biologist. That was a possibility to painful to contemplate since he loved it so much. He was also plagued by the thought that it might even ruin his wife's career. She worked for a prestigious research laboratory, also as a biologist, but was not as eager to push the boundary lines of nature with as much reckless abandon as he did.

He stayed down in the lab for days hunting for some clue in the books, some spark of an idea. Only when his wife incessantly buzzed him on the intercom to remind him to eat, did he stop and come upstairs to quickly wolf down some food so that he could get back to what he was working on.

The only thing he told his wife was that he was on the verge of a discovery. He instructed her to call the university and tell them he had the flu and, thus, would be out for a while. Little did she know that he had made the discovery weeks ago and he was now feverishly trying to figure out how to put the genie back in the bottle.

Down in his sub-basement, he tried out idea after idea, but the problem only became more unmanageable. It was clear to him that the track he was on was a dead end. He had to modify his thinking, but how?

ꝍꝍꝍ **Start solving!** ꝍꝍꝍ

The Price of Admission

Jon settled further down in his seat, trying to get comfortable as he struggled to keep watching the movie he was growing increasingly disinterested in. Having nothing much to do, same as every Friday night lately, he had decided to take in a movie at a theater close to his apartment. As Jon watched the movie, he imagined an adoring girlfriend sitting next to him, unable to concentrate on the movie, totally engrossed in Jon as she held his hand.

As he drifted along on the waves of this delicious and warming reverie, he thought he could hear a girl quietly sobbing somewhere behind him and it captured his attention. Jon tried to focus on the sound, hoping to zero in on where it was coming from. He turned his head to scan the faces of those sitting all around him, but in the darkness, he couldn't see too far

back. He tried several more times, but he still couldn't
see the sobbing girl.

His movements started to annoy those around
him and one man told him to sit still and let everyone
enjoy the movie.   Jon couldn't understand why
someone close to her didn't hear her sobs and try to
comfort her. He grew more and more obsessed with
finding this mystery girl, this stranger, this sad, sad girl.

Impatiently, he sat, waiting for a brightly lit
scene to throw some more light over the audience, but
when after more than twenty minutes that did not occur,
he decided to get up and slowly walk towards the back
of the theater. He thought that maybe as he walked, her
location would become more apparent to him.   Jon
slowly walked up the aisle, stopping momentarily at
each row trying to determine if he was getting any
closer to her.

When he had almost reached the back of the
theater, he spotted her and rejoiced at his good fortune

when he saw that the seat next to her was empty. Jon quietly lowered himself down into the seat beside her, trying not to look at her or startle her in any way. But, now that he had finally found her, now that he had finally achieved his goal, he was at a total loss as to how to approach her. Jon just sat next to her, listening to her sobs.

He took a sidelong glance at her, trying as discreetly as possible to find out whatever he could. She had beautiful eyes and seemed not to even realize that she was sitting in a theater amongst many people. She was totally lost in herself. Jon reached over, gently placed his hand on hers, and quietly whispered, "What's wrong dear heart. It can't be that bad. Please tell me. I'd like to help." Still sobbing, she told him that there was nothing anyone could do to help her, but when he persisted, she finally agreed to leave the theater with him and go back to her apartment down the block to talk. If he came with her to her apartment, he'd understand.

When they had arrived at her apartment, Callie offered him some coffee, and her mood seemed to lighten up just a bit and that made him happy. He felt like he had made at least some headway even though she still had not told him very much more personal than her first name. Jon tried to put her at her ease by telling her all about himself, the bad as well as the good. He persisted, trying his best to find out what was troubling her, but Callie wouldn't budge.

After awhile though, her mood seemed to become more pensive than sad and she drifted further away from him. Jon tried to close the gap by putting his arm around her shoulder, but she just responded by excusing herself to go into another room for a few minutes. Callie did not look at him. She just got up and walked away.

While she was gone, Jon, beginning to get hungry, thought he'd cut himself a piece of the cake she had put out on the table. But, as he started to cut the cake, he noticed that the knife looked like it had dried blood on it. She had probably used the same knife for cutting meat and apparently wasn't a very scrupulous cleaner. Jon was very particular about cleanliness, so he put the knife back down without cutting the cake, and just put his head back against the sofa, trying to formulate another plan.

When Callie did not return after a few minutes, Jon became concerned and called out to her a few times, but got no reply. Worried, he headed over to the other room and knocked on the door, but still he got no reply. So, now, really concerned, he opened the door, and gasped at the scene that lay before him. He could not believe what he was seeing. His mind could not grasp it, racing from one possible explanation to another, none of the explanations he cycled through able to put a check on his rapidly escalating heartbeat.

Callie was sitting at her dresser looking in the mirror smiling quietly to herself. Behind her, on the bed, was a young man lying in a dried pool of blood. The man did not move and, by the look of it, seemed to be dead.   Jon looked back over at Callie who had calmly picked up the phone to call someone.

He could feel the blood throbbing in his skull when realized it was the police she had called.   He listened, stunned, as she asked them, in a half hysterical voice, to quickly come to her apartment.   Callie told them that she had picked up a man at the movies, brought him back to her apartment, and he had gone berserk when her brother returned home, thinking it was her boyfriend or husband.   Jon was in such a state of panic that he could not hear the rest of what she was saying.

Finally, she hung up the phone, looked at him and smiled, then turned away and just stayed sitting at the dresser, quietly brushing her hair.   Jon thought of the knife and the blood he had seen on it.   Could that have been this man's blood on the knife that he had held in his hands only minutes before!   What a nightmare.

Should he wait for the police? Should he flee? Jon's mind reeled. He felt like time was running out. He had to figure a way out of this and in a hurry, but what could he do?

આ Start solving! ಲಲಲ

Going the Extra Mile

Eleanor stood at the back door of her client's house, key in hand, bracing herself for what she might find waiting for her today. She had spent the last nineteen years working as a housekeeper for the Adeline Cleaning Company and had always received high praise from her customers, all of whom had admired her thoroughness and conscientious devotion to her job. That is, until she was assigned to clean the Muldoon's house on Mondays and Thursdays.

After several weeks of working there, she had asked for another assignment, but was informed that no one else wanted this particular assignment either and that she was the only housekeeper the Adeline Cleaning Company employed who possessed all the particular qualities the Muldoon's had requested, not that Eleanor was told what these qualities happened to be. She found that odd, though, since both Mr. and Mrs.

Muldoon never seemed very pleased with her. But not wishing to make any waves with only one more year to go before retirement, she acquiesced, remaining as true as ever to her quiet, non-confrontational temperament.

And so, she took a deep breath, gathered up her energy, and proceeded to unlock the door. Eleanor had to put her shoulder against the door and push, in order to move aside the assorted boxes, newspapers, and other items that were heaped upon the floor by the door. Once inside, she looked around, trying to figure out where to begin. Even with all the cleaning she had done last Thursday, the house was in a lot worse shape than she had left it.

It seemed almost impossible that two people who were hardly ever home could manage to create so much of a mess. They were such intelligent, articulate, well-educated people that it didn't make any sense to Eleanor. Anyway, she resolved to do what she could to put things in order, laughing to herself that if anything could cure her of her compulsive cleanliness, this job could.

Eleanor rolled up her sleeves and proceeded to open up some of the downstairs windows trying to dissipate the pungent, chemical odor that always seemed to be in the air throughout the house. She could never manage to pinpoint the smell. It was everywhere. She busied herself, making neat piles of the boxes and newspapers, taking care not to open any of the boxes, as the Muldoons had instructed and reminded her incessantly. This was not easy for her since some of the boxes appeared to be leaking and she did not want to make more of mess of everything.

She contemplated finding some empty boxes to replace the leaky ones with, but just as she was about to start searching for some, the front doorbell rang. Eleanor knew it was probably a deliveryman, bringing the first of the Muldoon's usual Monday morning packages, which always came addressed to her, rather than to them.

More boxes! She signed for the new packages and turned her attention back to finding some empty boxes to replace the leaky ones with, but couldn't find any. So, she began opening up some of the boxes, hoping to possibly combine the contents of some of them.

Eleanor opened up the first candidate, her eyes growing wide as she stood looking down at the box's contents. It took all the force of her will to snap out of the shocked state of disbelief the sight had thrust her into. The box contained vials of some sort of liquid. There was no writing on the labels, just a rather scary looking collage of pictures. It looked to her like a muscular arm with a clenched fist, a skull, crossbones, and the symbol for infinity, all entwined together. Cautiously, she proceeded to open up some of the other boxes and found more of the same vials inside of them as well.

Feeling rather drained, Eleanor sat down in a nearby armchair, trying to make sense of it all. Her gut told her something was not right here. She tried to figure out what she should do, but what could that be?

෴෴෴ **Start solving!** ෴෴෴

Lost in the Shadows

Catherine slowly opened up her eyes, but since she was still feeling quite groggy and fatigued, she wasn't able to focus on anything. Her head ached and she couldn't remember the last time her body felt so heavy. She tried to sit up and as she did she became aware that her limbs were tied to the bed. Catherine pulled against the restraints, trying in vain to free herself, but after only a short while fell back onto the pillow, the effort having used up what little strength she seemed to have.

And so, Catherine quietly laid there, trying to take in her surroundings. There was a somewhat antiseptic odor hanging in the air that was horribly unpleasant. She wished she could cover her nose to escape from it, but the best she could do was to try to push it out of her mind.

Everything in the room seemed to be perfectly in place, but the room contained a rather odd mixture of items.   Against the wall in front of her bed was an expensive looking mahogany dresser on top of rested a tray with various medical supplies and instruments. To her left was a hospital bed covered with soiled, rumpled sheets, and what appeared to be some small, dried drops of blood. The paint on the walls was peeling in many places which made the ornate chandelier and immaculate looking Oriental rug seem out of place. On the other side of the empty hospital bed was a small, sparkling clean window, through which she could see the sun shining on the tops of some nearby trees.

The bed she was in looked to her like a hospital bed also, but the mattress wasn't very comfortable. It felt like there were hard, pointy lumps near the surface that pressed into her body and no matter which way she tried to reposition herself, they were always painfully present. Catherine tried feebly to get a handle on things, but her head was so foggy that she couldn't think clearly. She felt positively stuporous. She laid there for hours silently staring up at the ceiling, and then fell back into unconsciousness, only to awaken again several hours later. Over and over again, this cycle continued until three days later the door to Catherine's room finally opened.

Standing at the threshold was a tall, rather pleasant looking, clean cut man, dressed in the type of casual attire one would wear when relaxing at home. He was carrying a tray of food which he set down on the table next to Catherine's bed.

The man said nothing to her. He just remained calmly standing over her bed looking down at her face. The sight of him invigorated Catherine enough for her to muster enough energy to ask him what he thought he was doing by locking her up in this room. She continued on, in as strong a voice as she could manage, demanding that he undo her restraints at once.

The man completely ignored her protestations and did not respond. His face remained calm, but seemed somewhat saddened now by her remarks and the tone of voice in which she had spoken to him. After a minute though, she seemed to settle back down, so he proceeded with the task that had brought him up to her room.

He lovingly and patiently raised one spoonful of broth after another up to her parched lips which she willingly accepted. But, by the fourth or fifth spoonful, she was sure she tasted something really off about the soup. It was almost as if some of its ingredients had gone bad, but she wasn't really sure.

Catherine refused to eat any more. The man tried to coax her to keep going, but she only took one more mouthful which she planned to spit out at him, but at the last moment she looked into his eyes and because of what she saw there, just let the soup spill out of her mouth onto her bed clothing. She was in bed clothing. Clothing she did not recognize as her own. She had no recollection of how she had gotten that way.

Growing somewhat uneasy, he informed her that she needed to take some nourishment and to please reconsider, but she refused and turned her head away, moving herself as far away from him as she could get. This caused the man to change his tact and in same calm and soft-spoken voice as before, he inquired whether she was ready to acknowledge what she had done last week.

Catherine had no idea what he was talking about. She was still having trouble thinking straight and besides, she was starting to get sleepy again and was developing quite a stomach ache. When she pressed him to explain, he just looked totally crestfallen and told her that he couldn't understand why she was making believe she did not remember. With that said he turned on his heel and quickly left the room without giving her a chance to respond.

Catherine spent the next hour trying to think of what he could be referring to, but her mind was a complete blank. She did not even recognize this man, let alone remember what it was she was supposed to have done that he seemed so troubled about. The gnawing pain in her stomach was getting worse, and it began to frighten her. She knew she needed help, but what could she do? How could she extricate herself from this horrible predicament?

∾∾∾ **Start solving!** ∾∾∾

The Road to Hell

Jeffrey's wife Susan loved to cook and took great pride in the dishes she served to her husband for their evening meal. She had done this each night for the three years they had been married and he had grown accustomed to eating them. She had never had the opportunity to cook for him while they were dating since they had always eaten out at restaurants.

During their first year of marriage, Susan had also wanted to get up early to prepare him something he could take to work for lunch, but he had managed to convince her that even though he relished the sumptuous meals she prepared, he was obligated to have lunch with his colleagues and none of them brought their lunch from home. Even though Susan had thought it odd and rather extravagant that his colleagues never brought food from home, she had accepted it.

Now, this morning, she had placed a new hurdle in front of him. Just as he sat down at the table and was about to pour some cereal into his bowl, she gently whisked the box and bowl away and replaced them with a special breakfast surprise she had prepared for him while he was shaving. He looked down at the unappealing looking, yet perfectly arranged food on the plate before him and then up at his wife who was eagerly anticipating his reaction.

He took a bite, and loving his wife as much as he did, could not find it in his heart to say anything other than how absolutely delicious it was. He could see that she was pleased by this and thus tried to console himself with the fact that at least he had made her happy. He even managed to keep a smile on his face as he desperately tried to push the thought of tomorrow morning's breakfast from his mind and his growing intestinal troubles.

Things had been becoming more difficult lately though. Jeffrey had grown to love Susan more with each passing year and found it harder and harder to sidestep her cooking and the innocent lies he had told her. He had told her that her cooking was so much better than the finest restaurant fare. He had confided in her that her cooking was far superior to any of his colleague's wives cooking when in reality it was most likely the worst.

But the lie that was the hardest for him to live with was that her cooking was so good he couldn't resist a second helping. This had prompted Susan, who was eager to please him, to begin automatically filling his plate with double portions on a regular basis.

Jeffrey finished his breakfast, kissed his wife goodbye, and headed for the train station dreaming of the lunch he was going to have later with his colleagues. They were going out today to one of his favorite restaurants.

Once there, he ordered the cheese steak sandwich and fries he had been looking forward to all morning. Each bite was better than the last and he ignored the sidelong glances of his friends as they sat staring at him, completely spellbound by the way in which he was so enthusiastically devouring such ordinary fare and turning everyone's thoughts towards food. Finally, his friend Jason broke the spell when he started discussing next Friday's dinner party.

Jason had been pushing rather aggressively lately for this month's party to be held at Jeffrey's house. Unlike Jeffrey, he was a fellow who always spoke his mind, never holding back his feelings or opinions, always oblivious to how his words and blunt commentary affected those around him.

Everyone at the table, except for Jeffrey, had hosted a party numerous times. Jason would accept no more excuses from Jeffrey. The others, who had always given in to Jeffrey's somewhat creative explanations, now joined Jason in insisting the next dinner party be hosted by Jeffrey and his wife Susan. Even his best friend was now siding with the others.

Jeffrey suggested they break the mold and instead splurge and have a night out on the town with their wives. Why not take their wives to a fancy restaurant and a play this time? The suggestion was well received as an idea for the following month, but this month they insisted that Jeffrey had to pay his dues and host the dinner at his house. What was Jeffrey to do?

ح ح ح **Start solving!** *ﻮ ﻮ ﻮ*

Everything Old is New Again

Dyson repositioned himself in his easy chair, resting his head against its back and closing his eyes. He had polished off a rather large lunch and was feeling quite content and drowsy. As he drifted off, he thought how nice it was to be financially well-off, with the stresses of the work world long behind him. He could get up in the morning whenever he pleased. He could nap whenever he pleased.

His wife, Anna, was so happy with his success and early retirement. She adored him and he could think of no better companion to have. They had known each other since college where they had met while taking an economics course together. Anna had been amazed at the breadth of his knowledge on quite a vast array of topics and the ease with which he absorbed new material.

He had had a lot of friends until he retired, but then he had let those friendships fade away by never making himself available anymore.   Anna, never questioned this, but couldn't understand why since he had always seemed to be a people person.   Dyson had always relished the fact that he easily gained people's trust and confidence.   These days, though, he spent most of this time alone when he wasn't with her.

After Dyson had been dozing for awhile, he was awakened by the front door bell.   Being drowsy and not in the mood to get up, he decided to ignore the doorbell, but whoever it was persisted, mercilessly ringing the bell for several minutes.   Completely yanked away from his happy reverie, he finally got up, went to the front door, and looked through the peephole.

Standing there, looking somewhat anxious and impatient was a young girl, about ten or eleven years old.   Dyson opened up the door and before he could inquire what she wanted, she blurted out that she had come to buy the kittens that he had for sale and pleaded with him to tell her that he hadn't already sold them to someone else.

In as gentle and polite a manner as he could, Dyson informed her that he did not have any kittens for sale, but she did not accept his answer. The girl told him that she had spoken with his wife earlier in the day, but then had to go home to get the money to pay for them. His wife had mentioned nothing about this conversation and he started to think that perhaps the girl had remembered the wrong address. She began to cry, asking to speak with his wife. He conceded and opened the screen door, letting her wait inside while he went down to the basement to fetch her.

Once Dyson disappeared downstairs, the girl opened the screen door and stepped outside. She stood on the top step, twirling her hair until two middle-aged men got out of a car parked down the block a ways and walked up to her. The shorter, blond haired man gave her a kiss and instructed her to go on home. Both men then entered the house, closed the door, and proceeded into the living room.   They made themselves comfortable on the sofa, but did not unbutton their coats or even take off their gloves.   They just sat there patiently waiting for Dyson.

When Dyson came back upstairs with his wife, he got an uneasy feeling as he looked toward the front door that was now closed and the girl nowhere in sight, but he shrugged it off. He called out to her, but got no reply. So, thinking the girl had just decided to leave, his wife went back downstairs and Dyson walked towards the front door in order to lock it.

He got as far as the living room entrance before he noticed the two men. They were just silently sitting there, very still, staring at him, their faces betraying no hint of what they were doing there.   Dyson was stunned. A man does not expect to walk into his living room and find total strangers sitting on the sofa.

When he inquired, in as unantagonistic a tone as he could muster, what they wanted, they proceeded to tell him that they needed his assistance with something, chiding him for seemingly not remembering who they were and probably thinking that no one at the company had known how he had made his millions. They spelled out the details of what they wanted him to do.

They wanted him to explain the methods he had used to skim the interest calculated on customer accounts and show to them exactly how he employed those methods without detection, except by them of course. Dyson had put the past completely out of his mind when he retired, feeling that was the only way he would be safe from slipping up and saying something he shouldn't.

Slowly, he began to recollect their faces. They had worked in the company's audit department and his unit had been audited by these particular fellows on one occasion, but they hadn't reported any issues. No auditor had ever reported any issues related to his clandestine activities, just the usual 'keep better records about such and such', etcetera, etcetera.

What Dyson thought had been a secret all these years, that not even his loyal and adoring wife knew, had really not been a secret after all. Dyson sat down in his easy chair across from them, remaining very calm and cordial. He was mindful of the fact that his wife was almost done with the laundry she was doing down in the basement and would probably be heading back upstairs shortly. As they continued to speak, Dyson tried to figure out the best way to handle the situation, but what could that be?

ᕪᕪᕪ **Start solving!** *ᕬᕬᕬ*

Quiet Please

Kelly had always been a very friendly and lively gal with a very trusting nature. She was so inoffensive and welcoming that people were just naturally drawn to her. Over the years, her circle of friends had grown ever larger. This kept her quite busy. So busy, in fact, that she hardly ever got the chance to spend an evening or weekend by herself.

This weekend she had been invited to stay at her friends' country house. They weren't friends really. They were more like acquaintances. Both the husband and the wife seemed so nice, though, and she craved quiet so much, that she accepted their invitation without hesitation. Her friends' house was in a remote area and Kelly had visions of peace and relaxation.

This was not to be, however, since as it turned out, many other people were invited as well. From the moment Kelly arrived, they all began vying for her attentions. She didn't know why she had assumed it would be a quiet weekend in the country. Maybe it was just wishful thinking.

Mid-afternoon, Kelly decided she'd sneak out of the house to go for a nice, tranquil walk in the woods near the house. As she walked, she became totally immersed in the natural beauty all around her. She listened to the birds singing, marveled at all the many different shrubs and flowers, and followed a stream as it meandered through the woods, looking at the fish.

She had become so engrossed in her nature walk that she hadn't at all paid attention to what direction she had been walking. It didn't really hit her until she decided she had better start heading back to the house before her friends started getting worried.

Kelly tried to retrace her steps as best she could remember them, but finally came to the realization that she was lost. Worse than that, she was lost in the woods without her cell phone, without anything that could be of use to her. She had been so focused on escaping from the house guests that were crowding in on her that she hadn't even taken her purse.

Tired and hungry, Kelly sat down on a rock to rest and tried to think of what to do, but she couldn't seem to think clearly anymore. Kelly forced her mind to stay focused and, after awhile, decided the best thing to do would be to walk in a straight line until she came to a road or someone's home, hoping that she could get some help there.

With that strategy in mind, she set out with renewed hope and vigor. Coming up with an idea that seemed like it could work had given Kelly her second wind. Her anxiety subsided enough to let her mind wander back to her friends and the weekend at their country house. Many thoughts came and went until, suddenly, her mind came to rest upon a most horrible and paralyzing thought.

She remembered what her friends had said a few years ago when they bought the house. She remembered the reason why her friends said they never go out into the woods by their house. The woods were full of hidden traps and deep holes, put there a long time ago, and no one her friends were acquainted with seemed to know who had put them there or why.

Kelly was so annoyed. Why couldn't the townsfolk at least have marked the place with warning signs? She would now have to slow her pace and be on the lookout for these hidden traps and holes. This was something she did not want to do. Even worse, the light was starting to fade. So, she crept along. What choice did she have? At last, after what seemed like an eternity, she thought she saw her friends' house. Kelly was never so happy to see anything in her life.

When she got closer, she could see her hostess coming to greet her, smiling and scolding her in a friendly way for having left the house. Her friend stopped at the edge of the woods and stood there waiting.   Kelly turned and headed in her direction, distracted and no longer paying attention to her footing as she walked. She tried to hurry, as her friend seemed to be impatient.

Suddenly, the ground gave way underneath her and Kelly fell into a deep hole. Still full of happiness at having found the house again, she wasn't too bothered by the fall, and luckily for her, she hadn't broken anything.   She called out to her friend, but her friend didn't respond.

So, she patiently waited for her friend to come. Her friend had seen her fall and would be there shortly. Kelly was positive.   After fifteen minutes, though, Kelly started getting annoyed and began calling out to her hostess as loud as she could. She stood up and as she did, she could see a light coming toward her from above.   She was saved! When her friend finally appeared over the hole with the light, it shed enough light in the hole that Kelly was now able to see the area in front of her in chilling detail.   Kelly called to her friend to hurry up and help her out of the hole.

Her hostess replied flatly, "Why would I want to do that. I do want to thank you, though; you saved me a lot of trouble." Her hostess remained there above the hole, motionless, staring blankly down at her. The ball was now in Kelly's court, but what could she possibly do or say in her condition? What could she possibly do or say that would not make the situation any worse?

≈≈≈ **Start solving!** ✈✈✈

Off Hours Trading

Most of the time the trains got pretty crowded at rush hour, but this day it seemed even more packed than usual. Martin, glad to be sitting down, loosened his tie and unbuttoned the top two buttons of his shirt, then closed his eyes and tried to relax. He thought that maybe the reason why the car seemed so packed was because the air conditioning wasn't working well.

He tried to focus his mind on the happy thought that it was Friday and tonight, after a long, hard week of working at the stock exchange as a broker, he'd enjoy a nice quiet evening in front of the fireplace with his girlfriend. He was growing quite fond of her. She was so different from his last girlfriend who had filed, according to Martin, a totally unwarranted police complaint about him. His employer, he remembered, had not been very happy about it.

But try as he may, he couldn't focus on anything pleasant. Negative thoughts kept creeping in through the edges of his happy musings. Besides that, he was finding it difficult to breathe the increasingly hot, humid air that was filled with a dizzying array of sounds and smells.

Standing directly in front of Martin was a woman who, quite probably, hadn't bathed in a long time. Even worse, seated next him was a casually dressed, middle-aged man with rotten teeth busily eating his homemade breakfast from a plastic container. The smell was so pungent, yet unrecognizable, that Martin felt compelled to take a peek at the man's food though the corner of his eye, but it remained a mystery to him and was beginning to make him nauseous.

Martin looked around at the other passengers nearby. No one seemed the least little bit disturbed by either the man or the woman. They seemed content, quietly reading or dozing. They didn't even seem bothered when, at the next station, an obnoxious young man boarded the train. He was wearing a portable music player that was blasting music so loudly that Martin could feel it actually piercing his brain.

Since he couldn't relax, he hoped to distract himself from his surroundings by reading the fascinating book he had started the day before. Martin reached down into his briefcase to take it out, but as he did, he inadvertently banged his head against the smelly woman standing in front of him. The strength of the odor that smashed into his face was so overwhelming that he groaned and winced involuntarily.

When he sat back up, he could feel the eyes of the woman upon him. The woman was quite visibly upset and began talking to the man seated next to Martin, but she was speaking so quickly and excitedly that he could only make out pieces of what she was saying.

The man turned to Martin and asked him to apologize to the woman for what he had done. Martin didn't feel that he had done anything wrong. If anything, he felt that he was the wronged party, but not wanting to create a scene, he apologized to the woman in as polite a manner as he could muster under the circumstances.

Still upset, she did not accept his apology. Instead, she informed him that she was going to file a complaint against him and asked for his name, address, and phone number. A nearby passenger, overhearing the conversation and having apparently witnessed the incident, suggested that she not take him at his word and ask to see some identification. She should take the needed information directly off it instead. The passenger offered to be a witness in case she needed one in court. The man seated next to Martin said he would do the same as well.

To all of this, Martin shook his head in disbelief and said, "You'd think, by the way all of you are acting, that I had committed some terrible atrocity. For Pete's sake, all I did was bump into the woman. I apologized. This is getting ridiculous". Everyone stared at Martin, and increasingly more folks entered into the fray. Finally, one woman, who was at least six feet away from him, said, "You groped her and you think it's nothing!"

He did not want to hand out any personal information, but he was concerned about what the crowd would do if he refused to comply or tried to leave the train. What could he possibly do or say to defuse the situation?

&<&<&< **Start solving!** >->->-

Supernova

Mary Anne sat spellbound in the audience, looking up at Bryan, the lead singer of the alternative rock group 'Tomorrow is Today'. She was totally enthralled by his deep and throaty sounding voice. He was so handsome. She had watched the group's music videos over and over again, hoping that one day she'd be able to actually meet him in person.

Reading everything she could find on the group and especially, Bryan, she had discovered that Bryan had written most of the songs the group sang. In her mind, she slowly built a picture of what he must be like. Since his songs were so very dark and intense, Mary Anne imagined him to be the sensitive, creative genius type.

As the show progressed, it seemed to Mary Anne that Bryan's attention, so intense and sweetly disturbing, was increasingly focused on her. She could hardly believe it. Then, a fellow sitting at the table behind her leaned over to her and began whispering something in her ear.

Mary Anne lowered her gaze, staring down into her lap, as he continued his murmuring, as his words continued to weave their way through her brain. Before he had a chance to finish, not wanting to hear any more, Mary Anne moved her chair away from him to the other side of the table, still keeping her back to him.

Trying to recapture the mood, she looked up at Bryan, who was still focused on her, shifting his eyes only fleetingly to the whisperer behind her. But now, his face had a very different expression. Bryan's mood had turned gloomy. His eyes looked desolate and sad.

She couldn't help looking directly into them and slowly and deliberately mouthing the words, "I care. I care. I care", trying with all her might to push them into his psyche. That seemed to cheer him a bit, but only a very little bit. He jumped down from the stage, continuing his singing as he worked his way through the crowd until he was finally face to face with Mary Anne. Quickly, in an almost inaudible, but still commanding tone of voice, he invited her to meet him later after the show, to please meet him after the show. Then, in a flash, he was back on stage.

She turned to glare at the fellow who had whispered those terrible things to her, terrible and dangerous things about Bryan, things she just could not believe about him. He could not have been describing the Bryan she knew.

He returned her icy cold stare with a look of concern, a seemingly genuine concern for her well-being. This puzzled her. Why would he be concerned about her? He didn't know her. Was he trying to trick her? Was his motive sincere? What should she do?

෨෨෨ **Start solving!** ෨෨෨

Stay the Course

Alison had had a very long and busy day. Her husband liked the house to be in perfect order, with the rugs vacuumed daily, and everything sparkling. He usually became quite upset if anything was out of place, so Alison always worked hard to insure that it never was. Beginning to doze off in front of the television set, the first few minutes of rest she had had all day, she coaxed herself out of the chair to do one more chore before retiring upstairs to bed. She had made a habit, a good one she thought, of making sure that the house was locked and everything was off that should be off.

As she began to make her rounds, she noticed something peculiar on the floor. Alison couldn't recollect how it could have possibly gotten there. She looked around the floor and nearby counter tops and appliances, but she saw nothing else amiss. There was just this one spot of blood on the floor. And, it was still wet!

What struck Alison as even more bizarre was that it didn't have the look of a drop of blood that you might see if someone had cut themselves and dripped blood on the floor. This rather large drop resembled a perfectly formed square. She knelt down to have a closer look.

After inspecting it for a while and not being able to notice anything else about it, she decided not to let it worry her and wiped it up with a paper towel. She tossed the towel toward the trashcan, as she tried to put the event out of her mind. She was so deep in thought, however, that she didn't even notice that the towel had completely missed the trashcan. Alison turned out the light and went up to bed, alone, same as she did the many nights her husband stayed out late or tinkered in his workshop down in the basement.

At around 2AM, her husband, Mike, plopped himself down on the edge of the bed, intentionally awakening her.   Seeing the upset expression on her husband's face, Alison realized he must have detected something out of place.   She had seen that expression many times before and knew she was in for a long night.   But that was okay, she had gotten through it before, she'd get through it this time.

She complacently waited for him to speak.   She waited for what seemed like an eternity, but Mike said nothing.   He just sat there staring at her.

Then, it struck her.   She remembered where she had seen that same oddly shaped spot before.   It was last year, in the basement of their house.   Alison wished he would scold her or at least say something, but he remained silent.   He seemed to be thinking about something and not quite so upset anymore.

Finally, he spoke. "You saw it didn't you", he said flatly. At first, Alison was puzzled, but then she realized the implication of his words. Her heart pounding, she tried frantically to come up with an answer. But, what could she possibly say? What could she possibly do?

** festart solving! ฅ*ฅ***

Start solving!

Running at Full Speed

James sat back in his seat and stretched out his legs. He thought how nice it was to finally take a vacation where he could just kick back and relax. As the plane took off he could feel the stiffness in his neck subside and all the stress begin to drain from his body.

With nothing in particular that had to be done and no one pressing on him demanding his attention, James indulged himself in a little nap, sinking back into the pillow one of the stewardesses had given him soon after boarding he plane. It was not something he got to do very often. In fact, he couldn't remember the last time he had gotten a chance to really relax for more than a few minutes.

James worked as a doctor in a large city hospital that was having financial difficulties. It had kept him constantly on the go. Most days he barely had time to grab a bite to eat and he usually didn't leave for home until very late. Unfortunately, working double shifts had become second nature to him.

He hadn't take a vacation in years, but when he became so worn out that he started making some pretty serious mistakes, everyone knew it was time for him to slow down and take a respite from his grueling schedule. He was lovingly ordered to take a trip somewhere relaxing.

Knowing he was not the type to slow down, his co-workers confiscated all his little gadgets. They took his cell phone. They took his laptop computer. They even took his smart wristwatch. They wanted him to have nothing that would distract him from relaxing. So now, here he was, on a long flight to a sunny location and missing his gadgets less than he thought he would. In a few hours he would be basking in the sunshine and sipping margaritas.

After a nice little nap, James was starting to get hungry, so he looked around for a flight attendant. He thought he would inquire when lunch would be served, but there was no flight attendant in sight. That seemed strange, though, since it was quite a large plane. He thought there would be at least one flight attendant floating around in his area. He asked the other passengers nearby if they had seen a flight attendant recently, but they hadn't. So, since he was starting to feel a little bit cramped, he decided to get up, stretch his legs, and look around for one.

He searched all the areas that passengers were permitted to go, but there were no flight attendants anywhere, so he sat back down and absent-mindedly looked out the window and grumbled to himself about the poor customer service.

Since the plane was flying below the clouds, there were plenty of things on the ground to pass the time gazing at. However, when another half hour passed by with still no flight attendants in sight, annoyance turned into worry. What worried him even more, though, was that no one else seemed the least little bit troubled by it. He thought to himself, "I know my nerves have been frayed lately, but I'm sure something's wrong here".

James went up front to talk to the Captain. Since the door was locked, he tried knocking and calling out to Captain through the door, but got no reply which made him all the more agitated. He turned to the other passengers and said, "I think we are alone on this plane". They just gave him a brief, disinterested look, and then returned to whatever they had been doing before being interrupted. James knew something needed to be done, but what?

≈≈≈ **Start solving!** ≈≈≈

Forever Sorry

Rachel was nearing the end of many hours of shopping for her family and was becoming very weary of lugging around the increasingly heavy bundles, but she wanted to get one last item in the electronics department for her son. She thought she had just enough money left to pay for it. As she entered the area, two teenage girls raced by her, knocking her off balance. The loud thud her body made as it hit the floor was drowned out by the sorrowful sound her newly purchased dishes made as they shattered.

Tired and in pain from having banged her knee, Rachel calmly tried to pick herself up. No one was around to assist her, so she grabbed onto one of the counters for some support. The only salesperson in the area had his back to her, totally engrossed in rearranging some of the stock, and she was too embarrassed to disturb him. The girls, meanwhile, hadn't even stopped to see if she was okay, much less to apologize. They just came to rest in the distance and stood there staring at her, whispering back and forth to each other, and laughing.

Rachel, trying to ignore the girls, proceeded to complete her business in the electronics department. The store would be closing soon and she was happy, despite those terribly ill-mannered girls that she had managed to find everything she had looked for, even if her main purchase was now ruined. She knew her family would be pleased with the other items.

They hadn't been very happy with her lately, especially her husband, and she felt sure that some of these purchases would help to make them less annoyed. Rachel's husband had been particularly angry with her that morning and in keeping with her non-confrontational nature, she had left the house in the middle of his lecturing her about the stack of dishes she had broken while putting one of them away in the closet. The last thing she heard as she closed the door was her husband saying, "It's always something with you. It never ends".

On her way to the store exit, Rachel left the box of broken dishes near one of the poles without opening the box to assess the damage or even trying to get a replacement set from the store. She didn't think they'd believe her anyway. As she neared the door, still deep in thought, the sudden ringing of the store alarm and the security guard telling her to step to the side to have her purchases checked, snapped her to attention. She thought that a salesclerk had probably just forgotten to take the sensor off one of her purchases.

As she dug through her packages, looking for the offending item, she saw something in her bags that was not hers. Not only was it not hers, it still had its sensor attached. Since the guard had allowed her to rummage through her bags herself, only she was aware of it.

Rachel was in a panic over the discovery. She was afraid she'd be accused of stealing even though she felt positive that those girls who had knocked her down had done this to her as a sick joke. She began imagining the worst, feeling afraid that she would not be believed. And what would her family say?

Rachel looked up at the guard, who was becoming impatient and had a rather cold and forbidding air about him. She racked her brains trying to think of what to do. How could she get herself out of this horrible situation?

෩෩෩ **Start solving!** ෨෨෨

Seeing is Believing

Michael and his friends partied late into the night, trying to wring the last little bit of fun out their week long boat charter, paid for by Michael's parents as his college graduation present. The guys were happy they had decided to charter a boat, preferring it to the Caribbean cruise Michael's parents had originally suggested. They had the boat to themselves, except for the few crew members, two men and one woman, onboard to operate the boat.

Around 2AM, Michael, always the first one of the group to call it a night, bid his friends a good night and headed back to his cabin, as they teased him for being such as party pooper. On his way downstairs, he said goodnight to the crew, who all seemed to be a little bit drunk or stoned. He wondered how they allowed themselves to get this way while on duty and hoped their less than alert condition would not end up putting his friends and him in jeopardy.

Michael laid down on his bunk, closed his eyes and thought about his friend Josh, who always loved to play the clown, teasing him all day about the sharks that inhabited the area they were sailing in. Michael had spent the day staring periodically out at the water, looking for sharks, thinking sometimes that he spotted one or two in the distance, but never really sure.

He had just about drifted off to sleep when he heard his friend, Sam, start screaming that one of the crew had fallen overboard. He could hear him shouting to Jacky, the crewmember who had fallen overboard. Michael could hear his friends all panicking as he made his way back outside to where they stood, staring at the water, pointing a light in the direction of Jacky. Sam had thrown her a life preserver, but she hadn't grabbed a hold of it. She just seemed to be drifting in the water.

Michael tried to take charge of the situation. He directed Sam to try to find the other crew members, who were now conspicuously absent in this emergency, and have them bring the boat closer to where Jacky was in the water. It struck him as odd that she seemed so far from the boat, but he put that thought from his mind and focused his attention on rescuing her. Thank goodness it was a clear night, there was a full moon out, they had taken the sails down for the night, and they were only drifting in the water.

Then to his horror, Michael looked out at Jacky, who had now rolled over onto her face. Being the best swimmer of the group and knowing that immediate action had to be taken, Michael reflexively jumped into the water, as he called back to his friends to keep the light trained on Jacky so that he could clearly see where she was.

As Michael came closer to Jacky, he realized that it wasn't her floating in the water at all, but just a life size mannequin used for CPR training which had been dressed up to look like Jacky from afar. He turned to look back toward the boat, annoyed and upset at his friends, who were now gathered at the back of the boat, laughing their heads off. Jacky and one of the other crewmembers were standing next to them, looking equally amused. Josh shouted, "Hurry, she's going under!"

Michael headed back towards the boat, grumbling that he'd get even with them as he swam. The boat, however, never seemed to get closer to him. It always remained an elusive 50 yards away. They were having a rip-roaring time making him keep swimming, but it was late and he wanted to go back to sleep. So, Michael stopped where he was, remaining silently looking towards the boat, hoping that would make his friends tire of their game, come back, and pick him up. The boat did not stop. It just continued traveling further and further away with each passing moment.

Then, to Michael's amazement, he saw his friends move away from the back of the boat and go below deck. Michael tried to figure out what his next move should be, but what could it be?

❧❧❧ **Start solving!** ❧❧❧

Dropping a Stitch

Marguerite looked up from her sewing and turned her gaze toward her mother and sisters, sitting nearby, busying themselves with their daily routine. All five sisters were needed to help their mother make ends meet ever since their father passed away quite suddenly the year before. Each assisted their mother with whatever seamstress work she managed to get from the people that lived in their small and somewhat isolated town.

The doctors were never able to determine the cause of her father's death and her mother never pressed them for one. Neither did she cry at the funeral. She just picked up with her life and did what needed to be done for the family to survive.

Their work was very tedious and tiring, but if they worked steadily for long hours, they were able to

make enough money to keep food on the table, albeit
very modest fare. While her sisters worked, Marguerite
would often drift off into a daydream and at times she
would get so caught up in her reverie that her mother
had to scold her to get her back to working. Marguerite
did the least amount of work, but always complained
the most about her tired fingers and weary eyes. Her
mother seemed to have to push and prod her every step
of the way and was thankful that none of her other
daughters required as much constant attention as her
middle child, fourteen year-old Marguerite, needed.

This day, as Marguerite gazed out the window,
she spied a tall, very well dressed, rather formidable
looking man walking toward their home. As the
stranger came closer, she caught his gaze and smiled at
him, then recoiled at the icy, cold stare he gave her in
return. She wondered what business he could possibly
have with her family. She knew her mother was
worried about their being three months behind with the
mortgage and had been making them work longer hours
recently, sometimes until almost until bedtime. Was

this stranger a man from the bank, coming to evict them?

Her mother went to greet the stranger at the door and talked with him at the threshold for what seemed like an eternity to Marguerite. None of her sisters seemed interested. They just kept their eyes focused on their sewing, proceeding as usual with their routine.

After awhile, her mother and the stranger came over to Marguerite. Her mother told her, in an unusually matter-of-fact tone of voice, to go straight upstairs, quickly pack her belongings, and go with Mr. Danvers. Her mother offered no explanation and showed no emotion. Neither did the stranger, whom she now at least knew the name of. Marguerite just sat there stunned, totally bewildered. She glanced over at her sisters, who had now put their work aside and sat watching as Marguerite's horror unfolded before her. Marguerite implored them with her eyes to come to her aid, but they did not.

Her mother repeated her request, this time more forcefully. Marguerite could hear one of her sisters, Annie, quietly snickering and one of the others sisters, Catherine, say in a rather low and spiteful tone of voice, "You thought this was hard work? Now, you'll really see what hard work is. He'll be sure to get his money's worth. Mother said he paid quite nicely for you." A third sister, Teresa, chimed in, "The way I hear he works 'em, she probably won't even be able to last out the year before her body gives out." Only her shy sister Jenny, who always tried to avoid confrontations, gave her a sympathetic look, but still remained silent and did not come to her rescue.

Mr. Danvers, not wanting to waste time, motioned to someone beyond Marguerite's line of sight. Within moments, two young men, no older than seventeen or eighteen at most, came into the house and positioned themselves by Marguerite's side. Each young man took hold of an arm, helping to insure that she did not escape.

Finally, Mr. Danvers spoke. What he said sent Marguerite into a blind, desperate panic. He softly and smoothly said to her, as his eyes maintained that same icy stare, "You're mother's right. You're a pretty, young girl, indeed! But, our customers expect to get what they pay for. You'll do well to keep that in mind."

With that said, the two young men began to lead her upstairs to get her personal effects. Marguerite's mind was reeling. She knew she had to do something to extricate herself from this terrible predicament, but what could she do?

Start solving!

Squeeze Play

Liz was beginning to get impatient waiting for Emily to arrive, getting more and more annoyed by the minute. Emily had recently started working in the same department as Liz and Liz had tried to make her feel welcome. She invited her to lunch and gave her a tour of the neighborhood. She took it upon herself to show Emily the office procedures. She introduced Emily to her colleagues.

But, no matter how friendly Liz tried to be, Emily remained very cold and distant and her life outside the office remained a mystery. If Liz or any of her office friends made seemingly innocent inquiries of Emily, she would change the topic or walk away.

So, it was a surprise to Liz when three weeks later Emily invited her to go to the beach. She did not really want to accept, but thinking it might help to warm things up, she lied and told Emily she'd be happy to go, regretting her words even as she spoke them. To make the idea more palatable, Liz gently suggested that they invite some of Liz's friends to go along. Emily did not want to do that and so Liz, not being the confrontational sort, gave in.

They made plans to meet at a bus stop near the beach route at 10:00 Saturday morning. She felt embarrassed that she was dumb enough to accept, so she did not tell her friends or family about her plans.

Finally, after waiting quite a long while, Liz thought she spotted Emily, in the distance, walking towards her. She did not seem like she was in any particular hurry, which irked Liz all the more. Trying to make the best of what she anticipated was going to be a very long day, Liz managed to set aside her negative feelings and muster up a smile and a warm hello as Emily approached.

From the minute that Emily arrived, she was all sparkles and fun, telling one entertaining story after

another.   Liz   hardly   recognized   her.   She began
wondering if maybe Emily was just shy and went with
the flow of Emily's conversation, relieved that she
would not have to do all the talking herself.

As they continued waiting for the bus, two men
in an old, beat up car pulled up next to them. The men
were friends of Emily and offered to give them a lift to
the beach, which Emily accepted without consulting
Liz. When Liz did not move, Emily just chided her to
hurry up and get in the car, pointing out the bus fare
they'd be saving.

Liz did not feel comfortable about accepting a
ride from them and it struck her as odd that both men
were not sitting up front. One of them sat in the front
seat, while the other sat in the back. She did not want
to make a big fuss though, so she just hopped into the
back seat and the driver quickly sped off down the road.

Liz hugged the door on her side, trying to stay
away from the man in the back seat whose stare was

becoming increasingly uncomfortable. Emily kept on with her amusing stories as the men laughed and joked along with her. After driving along the bus route for five minutes or so, the driver turned off onto a small, dirt road saying that he knew a really good short cut to the beach.

As he did this, Liz could see the man next to her smile to himself. She asked him in a friendly way what he was thinking of that he found so amusing, but he did not reply. He just bid Emily to go on with the funny story she was telling, as he slid over in the seat until he was right next to Liz. She politely asked him to move back over to the other side, offering the lack of air conditioning as her explanation, but he did not comply. He just ignored her.

The road seemed to become more and more deserted the further they drove. There were no longer any houses along the side of the road, except for a few boarded up ones, here and there. Although she managed to show no outward sign of it, Liz was beginning to panic.

The whole situation did not feel right. Liz's mind began playing out all sorts of horrible possibilities. She tried to think of what to do. Was she just making a big deal out of nothing? She felt sure that her instincts were right and that she had to do something, but what could she possibly do or say that would not make things end badly?

ๆๆๆ **Start solving!** ๆๆๆ

The Sleeper Awakes

Life was never perfect for Anton, but he got by. And even if he never had what one could call a privileged life, at least he had been spared many of the hardships others had had to suffer. He had never known hunger. He had always had a roof over his head. He felt a sense of certainty about tomorrow. Each day of his life passed into the next without much variation. There were no surprises. He liked it that way. It was comforting.

So when three men came to his home and demanded that he go with them, he did not question why and he did not resist. He just went. He always found it easiest to go with the flow of things. It was safer. There was no time for notes, no time to take anything. They had to leave and they had to leave now.

The room into which he was thrown was totally empty. There was nothing, just the cement floor and walls. There was not even a window. And so Anton sat on the floor and waited. Hours past by and perhaps it was even days. He could not tell in the total darkness.

He just sat and quietly waited for 'it' to be over so that he could continue with his life. He did not know what 'it' was, but that did not matter to him. He would wait and get past it, whatever it was. He did not mind waiting. He was accustomed to it. The only difference was that he could usually occupy himself with some thing or other that needed doing, some task or chore to fill up the minutes. Here he could only wait. Wait and think, but think about what?

&~&~&~& **Start solving!** &~&~&~&

Not Worth Knowing

Nathan sat at the end of the bar, waiting for his blind date to arrive. He was positive the evening was going to be a total waste. His date had been described to him as easygoing, cheerful, intelligent, pretty, and doing very well at her job as a publicist. Complete exaggerations for his benefit, he was sure.

Nathan had come to the conclusion awhile back that his friends, all married and wanting him to follow suit, were starting to become like salespeople; show you enough samples, eventually you'll buy one of them. They never seemed to let up the gentle pressure on him, forever nudging him closer and closer to edge of the waterfall. He had gotten into the habit of automatically saying yes his friends' blind date proposals, navigating through each of the dates, each of the totally disastrous dates, as best he could. Nathan could never manage to say no to his friends.

Nathan took a sip of his third drink, thinking back on some of the more memorable 'mission marriage' assignments. Estelle was the first. She never stopped chattering, not even while she was chewing. She had never even noticed that he had barely said two words the whole evening. During dinner, just to see what she'd say, he started reading a book, pretending to become totally engrossed in it. It didn't phase her one bit. She just kept right on talking. Sadly, Estelle was up at the top of the list, one of his better blind dates. His head ached, just thinking about her.

His fifth date, Caitlin, was even more of an adventure. Before, if anyone had asked him if it were possible for someone to stare at someone else non-stop for an entire evening, he would have said no. After his date with Caitlin, he now knew that it was possible. Caitlin stared at him incessantly, although she did sometimes break the monotony by knitting her brow when he said something that did not make sense to her.

Once he realized that, he began to amuse himself by trying to see if he could get her to knit her brow every five minutes, right on the minute mark. He was very pleased with himself that he had succeeded at this self-challenge. That was the date's only high point for him. He had contemplated asking her out one more time to see if he could break his record with her brow knitting, shortening the time interval without arousing suspicion, but his friends set him up with another date before he could and he forgot about it.

His friends all seemed to like his blind dates and considered him too picky, never understanding why things did not work out with them. Nathan, though, did not believe himself to be 'too picky'. There just had to be someone better than the peculiar assortment of women they had wrongly thought so appealing.

He took another sip of his drink as he pondered what tonight's adventure might be. He looked forward to getting it over with, going home, and settling down in front of the TV to watch the late night movie with his dog, Tabasco, who he knew would be better company than tonight's wearisome date would certainly prove to be.

At last, she arrived and she was on time! That was certainly a new twist. His amazement, though, did not end there. She was pretty, cheerful, easygoing, and had quite a delightful sense of humor. She was just as lovely as his friends had described and more. Nathan was enamored.

He escorted Chloe into the restaurant area and asked the Maitre d' if they could have the quiet, little, out of the way table he spotted in the back. He felt sorry he had picked such a noisy, over-crowded restaurant, but he had made the decision based on past experience. Those types of establishments had usually helped him get the horrors of his blind dates over with quicker. Chloe had not been familiar with the restaurant and he sensed that she was not pleased although she said nothing about it.

Once seated at the table, Nathan could not stop staring at her. He never felt so awkward in his life. He did his best to make polite conversation, trying to tell her some funny stories and discussing the week's news events. Chloe, for her part, was so interesting and engaging that Nathan rapidly became hooked.

The only thing that disturbed him was that she seemed to be holding something back from him. Nathan inquired about this, telling her that she seemed distracted and asking her what was on her mind. She declined to answer him at first, responding only after he relentlessly pursued the topic.

She told him that Nathan's friends had clued her in as to his 'exploits', giving her all the horrifying details. She had asked to go on this one date with him because she was curious and wanted to see him in action for herself. Chloe told him that she had been sitting there trying to figure out what horribly embarrassing or degrading thing he had planned for her. Chloe was surprised by his charming manner that didn't quite fit with all the stories she had been told. He was really a very smooth operator she thought.

Nathan was dumbstruck. He realized that this turn of events was very bad - very, very bad. He had to do something to convince her that he was sincere, but how? What could he possibly do or say to make her realize that he really liked her?

≈≈≈ **Start solving!** *≈≈≈*

Round and Round it Goes

Melody lay in bed staring up at the ceiling. It was early and her husband Danny was still fast asleep beside her. She looked over at him, wishing she had his ability to sleep through anything. Things had been rough at work lately and try as she might, sleep seemed to elude her, the same as it had almost every night for the past few weeks.

Depressed by her grueling schedule, the seemingly thankless long hours on the job, and her recent poor performance review as a sales representative, she decided to do something that was quite unlike herself. She impulsively decided to take the day off and just have some fun, something her husband would not be too understanding about. So, when she kissed him goodbye, she did not tell him her plans for the day, but rather, just let him think she was headed off to work.

Once outside, Melody soaked in the sunshine of what was turning into a gloriously sunny day. She couldn't have asked for a better day to play hooky from work. Realizing that she hadn't called into her office yet, she stopped at an inviting looking outdoor café to get some coffee for breakfast and leave a message on her boss's answering machine.

Melody lied, reminding him that she would be going to a prospective client's site today and intentionally did not mention who the client was just in case her boss tried to track her down there. He was so busy and disorganized that Melody believed he'd just take note of it and never realize that she had neither mentioned it to him previously nor put it on the calendar.

Relieved that that was out of the way, Melody shut off her cell phone and tucked it away in her purse and proceeded to take a leisurely stroll down Harway Boulevard near the center of town. She enjoyed herself people watching and glancing in the store windows she passed by. She had been doing this for quite awhile, when she came across an intriguing clothing store she hadn't noticed before.

She was starting to get hungry, but decided to check out the store before finding a place to eat lunch. As she browsed through the racks, Melody thought she saw two sales clerks whispering to each other about her and she became uneasy. Her gut instinct was to leave. But when Jasmine, one of the sales clerks, came over to her with a big smile and a warm and friendly manner, Melody concluded that she was probably just imagining things and let Jasmine talk her into picking out some clothes to try on even though she hadn't really planned to do so.

Jasmine escorted her to the dressing room and pointed out which booth she should use, not allowing Melody to pick a different booth, one that was more brightly lit, even though the dressing room was empty. Melody acquiesced and went into the assigned booth as directed. She really didn't care though that the booth was too dim to see the clothes very well and that it was uncomfortably small because she didn't plan to buy anything. Besides, Melody hated confrontations and tried to avoid them at all costs.

Suddenly, as she was beginning to slip one of the dresses over her head, she was knocked aside as the mirror wall opened and someone grabbed her and pulled her behind the wall, covering her mouth and tightening the dress about her head so that she couldn't see what was happening. She was dragged for quite a long distance and when they finally came to a stop, she could feel duck tape being wrapped around the dress near her neck and top of her head.

Terrified, Melody screamed that she couldn't breathe and was relieved when a small slit was cut in the leather dress near her mouth. Her attacker then proceeded to instruct her, in a very mechanical sounding voice, that if she tried to rip or remove the dress from her head, she would be killed without hesitation. She started screaming again, but all she got in return was laughter.

Melody pleaded with her attacker, trying to find out who this horrible assailant was and what he or she wanted, but she got no response. She could not even tell if there was more than one of them. All she could hear was a faint, muffled crying in the background and after awhile, the sound of several people moving about. An unfamiliar and very unpleasant odor pervaded the air. It was beginning to make her nauseous and somewhat light-headed.

Through the slit by her mouth, she could tell that it was light inside the room, so she began to push at the slit with her jaw, trying to stretch the leather out enough to enable her to see part of the floor through it, but she was unsuccessful. Failing at that, Melody, trying not to panic, decided her best bet would be to find an opening in the wall somewhere, so she proceeded to walk in a straight line until she finally hit a wall and then began to feel her way along it.

The wall felt like it was made of glass and now that she was close to it, she could hear the muffled sound of voices on the other side. Hope welled up inside her as she started pounding on the glass, crying out to them for help. She was at it for less than a minute when she stopped, becoming totally dazed by what she heard one of her hoped for saviors say rather loudly and gleefully, "Looks like she's gonna be a real fun one to watch. I hope she lasts longer than the little weakling they had last month."

Frightened and now physically drained by the unbelievable comments she had just heard, Melody slid down the wall to the floor, curled up into a ball, and tried to calm herself down. Even though the situation seemed hopeless, there had to be some way out of this nightmare, but what could it possibly be?

❧❧❧ **Start solving!** ❧❧❧

Zeroing In On Success

Today was the big day Jack had been waiting for. He had been patiently preparing for this day for a long time now. By 11 AM today, he would know whether his ideas would be accepted and whether the group would begin implementing the changes he envisioned. He marveled at how simple, yet elegant his plan was.

Jack looked over the conference table, eyeing the decoy meeting materials he had placed at each seat around the table. Seeing that everything was perfectly in place, Jack walked to the back of the room and just sat quietly next to the projector until the meeting time arrived.

He had handpicked each attendee after making a very careful study of their backgrounds. None were executives or even managers. He had concluded that all of them were ambitious, but were followers, not leaders. All performed different functions within the organization. None knew any of the others. None knew Jack. They only knew that he was higher than them in the organization and had a reputation for success. He couldn't ask for a more perfect group of individuals to help him with what he felt was a risky, yet very necessary undertaking.

Finally, it was time. He watched intently as each attendee solemnly entered the conference room and took their designated place around the table. For several minutes after everyone had arrived, Jack remained motionless, saying nothing. One brave attendee, Vincent, joked about it, but Jack glared at him in such as way that the gentleman stopped mid-sentence and looked away, trying to avert Jack's gaze. All the others followed suit.

After what seemed like a long enough time, Jack turned on the projector and displayed his first slide and then the second, third, and fourth, projecting each slide in turn as his audience sat staring up at the screen in stunned silence. The slides depicted in detail, the previously secret and unlawful indiscretions of each of the attendees. They kept rolling past until finally, the main part of the presentation, the reason they had all been gathered together, began.

Jack spoke. His voice was as flat and expressionless as his face. His words flowed without effort. He made it clear to his audience that he expected that they would be agreeable to his planned changes in production and would begin putting them into action at the conclusion of the meeting without delay. Jack then proceeded to outline the changes they were to help implement.

As Jack delved further and further into the details of the plan, the attendees squirmed in their chairs, as the growing sense of horror and dread made it increasing more difficult to breathe or even think clearly. Their visions of career advancement faded. None of them had known what to expect, but they certainly did not even in their wildest daydreams anticipate what was unfolding before them. Each felt it would be a calamity, not only for the organization, but also for those who would innocently purchase these new products. The damage would be irreparable. Hopelessness hung palpably in the air.

Suddenly, Tremain pounded his fist upon the table, calling for the others to ignore Jack's request and not to listen anymore. This surge of courage and leadership took Jack by surprise. From his studies, he had concluded that Tremain was a quiet fellow, who kept to himself most of the time. Jack responded by suggesting, for the sake of Tremain's children, that he calm down. His children's safety depended on it. If he had to use scare tactics to spur people into action, it was unfortunate, but he knew this mission was too critical, too vital to everyone's well being, to allow anyone to throw things off track. He had to do whatever it took.

Jack felt frustrated that the team did not seem to grasp the gravity of the situation and the importance of the mission. It was imperative that everything be in place within the next few days and Tremain's role was at the very center of the plan and vital to its success. Since Tremain was the smartest of the group, he had been assigned the most precarious part of the plan.

The other attendees remained silent. No one spoke up to support Tremain, who eventually quieted down, but was still visibly shaken. Jack looked at each of the attendees, one by one, asking each one individually for their pledge to put their piece of the production changes into action. Each one gave their word to do so, some without hesitation, others only after some prodding. In the end, they all acquiesced, even Tremain.

Jack then proceeded to dismiss the meeting, reminding them that the plan was to be kept strictly confidential. No one, not even their families, could be told about it. As Tremain passed Jack on the way out, Tremain smiled at him, making apologies for his behavior at the meeting, and whole-heartedly restating his pledge to faithfully execute his piece of the plan. Jack needn't worry. Jack could rely on him.

Jack remained behind in the meeting room, Tremain's outburst weighing heavily on his mind. The meeting hadn't gone as well as he had expected it would. He had hoped that when he outlined the urgency of his plan that all the attendees would rally around it without needing to be forcefully convinced of its merit. He had been so confident of his analysis. He still was. His resolve remained firm. He knew his plan must proceed. What should he do now, if anything? How could he ensure success?

అఎఎ **Start solving!** ఇఇఇ

One Toe over the Line

Mr. Mason's son, Andy, had always been a very popular boy. Never a day went by when he didn't have at least one or two friends over the house after school or some friend inviting him over to their house. He was considered the leader in his fifth grade class and all the kids flocked around him during recess. He never gave his parents a moment's worry, always full of optimism and cheer, never causing any upset.

It had been like this right from the start. The kids he'd meet each new school year would become instant friends with him and after awhile they would look up to him just as the others before them had. Andy was lucky that way. Neither Andy nor his parents knew exactly what it was that made the others gravitate towards him. They had their theories about it, but mostly they were just happy that it was so.

The Mason family was very content with their life together. They were comfortable financially and every one was healthy and well. So, when they unexpectedly inherited a sizeable sum of money, they decided to splurge and treat themselves to a total home makeover. The Mason's had barely changed a thing in the house since before Andy was born.

They decided to hire Junie Harper to assist them with replacing practically everything, from the wallpaper to the furniture, down to even the rugs on the floor. Junie was a local decorator, newly graduated from design school, and chocked full of ideas and enthusiasm. She was given a generous budget and free reign to do as she thought best.

The only caveat she was given was not to touch anything in the basement. It was to be left completely as it was now and not disturbed in any way. Mrs. Mason even told Junie to make sure that the workmen did not venture down there for any reason, to guard against them accidentally putting the basement out of balance. Junie thought this a rather odd request, but in the short time since she had started her own business, she had already dealt with a number of eccentric customers and stranger requests than this, so she promised Mrs. Mason that she'd comply with her wishes and did what she could set her mind at ease in this regard.

A few weeks later, after all the work was completed, Andy came home from school very upset. When Mrs. Mason finally got Andy calmed down enough for him to explain what was the matter, he told her that everything had gone horribly wrong that day. The kids in school no longer looked up to him as their leader. That honor was now Michael's, a new boy in class. In addition, his teacher had given him a 'B' on his writing assignment. He had never received anything less than a perfect score before. Alarmed by this news, Mrs. Mason went down into the basement and to her horror discovered that the basement was now out of balance.

Two days later when Junie came to the house to collect her final payment, Mrs. Mason cornered her and demanded an explanation as to why the basement had been disturbed. Junie apologized and suggested that although she hadn't witnessed it, one of the workmen might have gone down into the basement against her orders. Trying to humor Mrs. Mason and keep things friendly so as not to jeopardize receiving the final payment from the Masons that she was relying on, she offered to help set things right. Mrs. Mason's glaring look instantly turned into a hopeful smile and she accepted Junie's offer. She began herding Junie towards the basement door so Junie could begin assisting her without delay.

As Junie walked toward the basement door, she turned back to look at Mrs. Mason and she saw that her face had now taken on a cold and determined expression. Becoming scared, Junie tried to make an excuse about being late for another appointment, promising to return later in the day to help, but Mr. Mason, now on the scene and completely blocking her path away from the basement entrance, chided her that she owed it to them to set things right. In a total panic now, Junie knew she did not want to go down into the basement, but what could she say, what could she do, not to make the situation any worse for herself?

∾∾∾ **Start solving!** ∾∾∾

The Incessant Contestant

Margaret had never won anything before. She played the lottery on occasion, but never won even the lowest prize. For years, she bought raffle tickets, entered mail-in and radio contests, but lady luck never smiled on her. So, she was quite excited when, to her surprise, she won the essay contest she had entered. Of all the contests she could have won, this was the least likely one in her mind that she could possibly win. The fact that she not only won, but won the grand prize, a transatlantic cruise, was more than she could grasp.

For the contest, she had had to write an essay, in the form of a letter to a government agency, persuading them to change some policy. She had entered this particular contest just for the fun of it. She never expected to win it! Persuasion was not exactly Margaret's long suit. In fact, you could say she was rather bad at it. She couldn't even get people to do simple things, let alone get them to make changes to government policies.

As her excitement wore off, the realization that she had won a cruise began to sink in. Horror was more like it. Margaret was deathly afraid of the water. She tried to give the ticket away to friends and relatives. They only told her that it was a once in a lifetime opportunity she could not pass up. In the end, they persuaded her to go.

After several days at sea, Margaret's fears got the better of her. Everyone around her was having fun. They relaxed in the sun. They played games. They partied. Margaret, however, only worried about all the things that could go wrong. She worried about small things. She worried about horrible disasters. She worried about everything.

Her fears so overwhelmed her that she constantly annoyed everyone with her doom and gloom what-if scenarios. It got to a point where none of the passengers would talk to her anymore. Even the crewmembers would politely listen to her when they couldn't avoid her and then escape from her as quickly as possible.

Finally, she made up her mind. She felt certain disaster was going to strike and she was going to be prepared. She started by trying to become as familiar with the ship as she could. She explored every nook and cranny and even snuck into the areas that passengers were not supposed to go. She came upon a remote storage area that seemed dusty and long ago forgotten.

In this place, she found lots of old and fascinating items. She got so caught up in browsing through them that her fears started to melt away. That's when she spotted it. What she saw was way beyond any horror she had imagined.

She saw what appeared to her to be a timer attached to a device she did not recognize and it was counting down. The timer was at the 4 hours and 15 minutes to go mark. Margaret was certain all her fears had been realized, that she was probably staring at a bomb of some kind even though by appearances it didn't look like one, except for the timer.

She knew she must warn everyone, but what could she possibly say, what could she possibly do to persuade them that she was not just imagining things?

ๅๅๅ **Start solving!** *ๆๆๆ*

Two Plus Two Equals Five

It was the first day of class and Anna Marie made sure to leave the house early so she could have everything all set up in the classroom before her students arrived. She couldn't be more happy or excited at the new start that had been offered to her. Her last teaching assignment had not gone well and she had been asked to leave. The school had not found her 'radical teaching method' suitable. Even though she did not agree with their assessment of her approach to teaching, she did not protest when they terminated her employment.

This new school, the Madison Academy for Gifted Children, she thought would be different. She had already met with the parent council and they seemed very receptive to her ideas, even welcoming what they saw as a ray of hope for their school, which was beset by a wide range of behavioral problems.

Although they didn't quite comprehend Anna Marie's approach, the school, as well as, the parents most of whom were leaders or pioneers in their fields, agreed to give her the freedom to create her own syllabus for her eleventh grade chemistry students. Thus, she left her house with several shopping bags of stuff for her students and a heart full of enthusiastic anticipation.

When she arrived at her classroom, she placed the items from all but one of the shopping bags strategically around the classroom. The last shopping bag, which contained a sealed box, she placed on a low table in the front corner of the classroom opposite the door in plain view of all the students. Next, Anna Marie proceeded to inspect her classroom, making sure the keys for the door locks worked, the windows shades functioned, and the three-way light switch was operating properly.

Anna Marie was just finishing her preparations as the first students began filing into the classroom and taking their seats. One by one, the students became aware of what she had written on the blackboard. Most of them just sat in their seats, very still, mouths agape, in a state of stunned disbelief. Others glared at her, clenching their fists under the desk, and thinking that she had no right to do such a thing to them. And then there was Hamilton, who was the shyest, but had the highest IQ out of anyone in the class. He just sat quietly looking about the classroom assessing the situation, trying to figure out if Anna Marie could possibly be serious.

When the last of her students had entered the classroom, Anna Marie locked the door and pointed with the tip of her ruler to what she had written on the blackboard: "The passing grade in this class is 65. You will be assigned extra homework for every 5 points you score above that on any examination. If the homework assignments are not handed in on time and done to my satisfaction, 10 points will be deducted from your final average for each occurrence. There are no exceptions to this rule. This rule is not open for discussion."

She then proceeded with their first lesson, discussing the lives of some of the pioneers in chemistry. When there was about 15 minutes to go until the end of the period, she asked them to put their belongings under their desks except for a blank sheet of paper and a pen. They would take their first examination now. For the test, they had to look at the ten numbered items she had placed around the room earlier and name the item and at least two of its properties. She then let them know that this evening's extra homework assignment was in the shopping bag she had placed in the front corner of the room earlier.

The items were so common that they would all be able to achieve a perfect score without any effort. It seemed that they just had to decide what their grade would be and how much extra homework they were willing to do. The extra homework, they surmised, would probably be as easy as this ridiculously simple test.

Everyone but Hamilton decided they would answer all the questions correctly. Hamilton had another plan, but what could it possibly be?

න්නැන **Start solving!** ෨෨෨

A Turn of the Wheel

Alicia and Janie had been neighbors and friends for the last three years. Each Saturday morning, in an effort to stay in shape, they would go jogging together before breakfast. While having radically different political philosophies and mostly different interests, they both shared a passion for health and fitness, taking pride in staying in good condition and preparing healthy meals. It was from this that their friendship developed and they eventually fell into a comfortable routine of spending many Saturday afternoons together.

This particular Saturday, Alicia thought it would be fun to rummage through 'The Treasure Chest', a large outdoor flea market in the next township. They had never been there, but Alicia had heard they could find fabulous bargains on second-hand items and unique treasures garnered from various estate sales.

Janie promptly agreed with Alicia's idea for their Saturday afternoon, as she invariably always did. It was a quality that Janie's husband Charles and many acquaintances found pleasing at first. But they soon realized that she always did just as she pleased in a passive, non-confrontational kind of way. Being like-minded in most ways, as well as being very demonstrative and assertive people, both Alicia and Janie's husbands found this aspect of her personality most annoying.

When Alicia and Janie arrived there, they could swear the flea market had been misnamed. It looked more like a vast junk yard. There were various worn out odds and ends all jumbled together with seemingly priceless antiques. A person could wander through this mesmerizing maze of cast-off possessions for hours and not even see a fraction of the many vendors' offerings.

As Janie looked at the different items, she tried to imagine who the previous owners might have been, what their life was like, and what made them decide to give the item away. Had they died and their lifelong accumulation of belongings and little treasures then gotten sold to this or that vendor. Alicia, though, did not share Janie's active imagination. She was more interested in finding a good bargain and Janie's incessant musings were becoming tiresome, but she managed to keep her annoyance to herself.

Alicia shepparded Janie around for a couple of hours, skillfully directing Janie's movements through the maze of vendors. Janie thought it odd that some of the vendors seemed so friendly to Alicia, like old pals. Finally, Alicia convinced Janie it was time to head home, and directed her down a narrow passageway toward the parking lot, but just as they were nearing the end of the passage, Janie spotted the one item she just had to purchase.

Several yards away, set off by themselves, pristine and perfectly arranged on a shiny silver tray, were a set of cobalt blue perfume bottles. They had such an intricate design that Janie was sure they must have been at least a hundred years old, if not more. Janie couldn't believe her good fortune. The merchant only asked twenty dollars for the entire set because this was her last day selling at the flea market and she was trying to sell off as many of her wares as possible.

While Janie got into the front seat, Alicia placed Janie's purchase in the car trunk. Janie didn't mind how long it seemed to take Alicia, happily thinking that Alicia was making sure they were nice and secure. Janie was ecstatic and dismissed Alicia's comments when she got in the car about what a waste of money the bottles were. Alicia condescendingly remarked that Janie had so many of them already and that they were probably made last year in some factory, hardly worth the twenty dollars she paid for them.

As soon as Janie got home, she set them on her bedroom dresser and emptied the contents of her plain, old perfume bottles into them. She enjoyed the feeling of spraying perfume from them, covering her neck and arms, and filling the air with a mixture of delightful smells. Her perfume seemed to have such a different aroma when sprayed from these beautiful little bottles.

Lost in her musings, she totally forgot about getting ready for dinner, and only remembered when her husband Charles came home and walked into the bedroom. Seeing her sitting there, not yet ready as usual, he pushed her to hurry up and quit daydreaming in front of the mirror, and did not even notice her new acquisition.

Jamie started to get up, but as she did she noticed that her legs felt somewhat tired. She shrugged it off and got changed to go to her favorite restaurant. As the meal progressed, Janie felt more and more sleepy and her legs were becoming so heavy that she could hardly move them to cross her ankles. When she began slurring her words, she really became alarmed.

Janie was about to mention her concerns to her husband, but then thought he seemed oddly oblivious to it all. She had practically stumbled out of the car and he hadn't said a thing. Charles was just looking at her, cool and calm as could be.

She stopped conversing and just sat quietly as he continued speaking of the day's events. It occurred to her that her symptoms started as soon as she had used the new perfume bottles she had brought home from the flea market. Janie, no longer able to contain herself, blurted out to him that she thought she had been poisoned and proceeded to tell him as best she could of the details of what she was surmising about the perfume bottles.

Charles let her continue on for awhile, but then interrupted her monologue, first assuring her that he loved her, and then telling her that he didn't feel he could take much more of her active imagination, that she was wearing him out. He felt frustrated that the evening wasn't turning out as he had hoped, but he managed to suppress his anger and proceeded to quietly plead with her to take hold of herself.

Janie replied that if he wouldn't help her, she'd call for an ambulance herself and motioned to the waiter to come over. Charles could see the waiter approaching their table. He knew he needed to do something to keep the situation under control. He did not want any interference from the emergency medical response team or worse, the police. He needed to think of something fast, but what could he say or do to defuse this situation?

Start solving!

Final Notice

Patty just sat there. She just sat there staring at all the bills, all the overdue bills. There was no money to pay them since she had been laid off from her job some time ago. Recently widowed, Patty barely had enough money to keep her two young children fed these days. Her youngest was barely out of diapers. And, as if the past few years had not been hard enough, today she received the final notice to pay the mortgage on her house. The thought of her and her children out on the street was more than Patty's already frazzled nerves could take. At one time, the job offers had poured in, but these days, employment seemed nowhere to be found.

She had long since exhausted the kindness of all her friends and neighbors, who now tried to avoid her. Even Mr. Hamilton, the neighbor with whom she shared a common driveway, had become especially adept at it. No more cheerful morning greetings. No more after dinner coffees in the backyard together. No more weekend barbeques. Now she could see him sneaking a peek out the window to make sure the coast was clear before leaving the house. He had become very furtive.   Mrs. Hamilton was even better at it. In the past, she could always be seen around the property, hanging the laundry out to dry, gardening, or doing some other household chore. Patty hadn't caught so much as a glimpse of her in quite some time.

They had abandoned her.   Patty did not like that. In fact, in made her mad. She had always given them a hand when they needed it. She never even gave it a second thought when they asked for something. She had run errands for them, helped them remodel their house, and had gladly lent Mrs. Hamilton money whenever she ran short for the week. She had been their friend. A good friend she thought. She even used to sit for hours sometimes, comforting Mrs. Hamilton after she had had a fight with her husband. Now Patty needed them. Patty glanced down at the mortgage bill and thought about her friends. She decided they needed a little wakeup call on the meaning of friendship, so she headed out the door to go over to her neighbor's house.

Patty rang the bell, but no one answered. She peered through the window panel alongside the door to try to see if they were at home and just not answering the bell. She could see Mr. Hamilton sitting at the kitchen table eating his lunch, and thought she saw him look up and then quickly shift his gaze away from her direction. Getting more irritated, she kept ringing the bell, stopping only briefly to pound on the door, before resuming her bell ringing. When she still got no response after five minutes, she walked around to the back of the house, muttering to herself and rubbing her now sore hand as she went.

Mr. Hamilton was waiting for her at the back door. He smiled, but Patty could see by his manner that he was anxious to get rid of her. She forgot all about the friendship speech she had planned to give them. Patty dove right in. She didn't dance around the edges;

she didn't offer any explanations. She simply said, "I need some money to help with the bills. I always lent your wife money when she asked. Now I need some. What do you say?" Mr. Hamilton, trying to control his temper, ordered her off his property.

Patty, who was determined not to be so easily dismissed, demanded to speak with Mrs. Hamilton, pointing out that she had been doing a fine job of hiding herself lately. Her neighbor's face went white. Patty thought it an odd reaction, but pressed on, demanding to speak with her. She kept pressing and pressing, until finally Mr. Hamilton explained in a rather quiet and calm voice why Patty could not speak with Mrs. Hamilton, why she had not been around lately. She had passed away quite suddenly.

Patty felt ashamed. She apologized to Mr. Hamilton, gave him her condolences which he accepted, and turned to leave. As she did, she happened to look out toward the back of the yard and saw a mound of dirt where Mrs. Hamilton's Rose bushes had been.   The Rose bushes Mr. Hamilton had always hated.   There were no more Rose bushes, just a mound of dirt.   She turned back toward Mr. Hamilton and was about to ask him about it, but she saw that he was now looking back there also, and had a somewhat nervous expression on his face.   His gaze then shifted towards her and he smiled.

Patty could feel her throat tighten, her feet firmly glued to the ground.   Patty was sure Mr. Hamilton had done away with his wife. He had joked about it often enough.   She tried hard to think of something pleasant to say, something distracting. Maybe he didn't think she suspected.   Maybe she was making too much of the expression she had seen on his face.   But, what if she was wrong and he really did suspect?   She could feel her legs growing weak.   What should she do?   What could she do?

෴෴෴ **Start solving!** ෴෴෴

Appendix A

Ideas for taking *Outsmart the Unexpected* beyond
the borders of the book

1. **Throw an 'Outsmart the Unexpected' Party!**
   Invite your friends and/or relatives over and have
   one of them read the story to the group. Designate
   the amount of time everyone has to come up with
   possible solutions and the rules of the road (maybe
   the rule is no rules). You can do it as individuals or
   divide up into teams. Once done, debate and
   discuss the solutions you came up with. Maybe
   even determine how the group will decide which
   solution is most and least likely to be successful.
   Hmm, maybe even think up some interesting
   honors or 'surprises' for the best and worst
   solution.

2. Host an "Outsmart the Unexpected" Improv Night.

Sit in a circle and have someone read the story to the group, then rather then coming up with a solution to the predicament at the end of the story, have everyone take a turn at carrying the story one step further. Take the story as far as you can and see what you come up with. Maybe keep the lights low to make the setting more relaxing and help to stoke everyone's imagination.   You can even split up into teams and compare where each team ended up.

3. **Exchange and Debate Solutions in an Online Chat Session**

Set a time and location to chat online and post it - inviting anyone who wants to get in on the discussion. Maybe schedule a chat each week to discuss a different one of the stories.

4. **Create an Online Discussion Group**

Set up online discussions for each story and maybe organize by (a) most inventive solution, (b) plan B solution (always need one of those!), (c) most out there 'on the edge' solution, (d) most daring. You get the idea.

5. Hold an "Outsmart the Unexpected" CSI Event

Initiate a debate to explore how the predicament the characters are faced with could have happened in the first place! Was it fate, luck, decisions made? For example, can making sure your shoe laces are tied really protect you from falling objects?

Made in the USA